SILENT HARMONIES

A JOURNEY THROUGH HIDDEN FEELINGS

A Poetry Collection By

KARAN SAMRAT

SILENT HARMONIES

A Journey Through Hidden Feelings

Edition: Sept 2025
ISBN: 978-93-344-2175-0
Edited & Designed by: Smt. Aashwika A. Misra

MESSAGE FROM AUTHOR

Every book has a heartbeat, and Silent Harmonies: A Journey Through Hidden Feelings is no exception. This journey began not just as a collection of words, but as a reflection of the countless emotions we all carry within us — love and loss, joy and sorrow, silence and unspoken dreams.

I owe my deepest gratitude to my parents, whose endless sacrifices and blessings became the roots of this creation. To my beloved wife, who stood beside me with faith and patience, and to my siblings, my forever companions, who filled this path with encouragement and warmth. Without their love, this book would have remained just an idea.

The story behind this book is not mine alone — it belongs to everyone who has ever fought silent battles, celebrated hidden joys, or longed for words to express what their heart feels. Each poem, each line, is inspired by real human connections, by the struggles and triumphs that make us who we are.

TABLE OF CONTENT

MY DADDY IS A SUPERHERO

When she was dropped by her office Van,

She was going through a lane,

When she heard a sound weird,
She started shivering with fear and pain.

She got today late and missed her last bus,
But now it's dark and weird voices in universe.

She started moving fast,
And praying to the god,
Just save me this time,
Next time for overtime I won't stop.

Suddenly dogs started crying,
Owl started making weird sign,
She looked back and checked her path,
Is there someone following her in the dark?

She was missing her dad badly,
As this darkness seems to be deadly,
Her father always protected her like a guard,
Without him living like this was so hard.

She found that someone is following her,
She checked her phone that was showing a network error,
She thought now her last time came,
She stood like a pause in a video game.

Suddenly someone came her around,
She got scared and about to fell on ground,
But that shadow caught her well,
And said dear I won't ever let you fail.

I am here to be with you,
Baby open your eyes papa loves you,
She was now okay to be with her dad,
Now she was feeling safe and protected.

When she reached home she looked back her,
To invite her dad to have some dinner,
But then suddenly someone called her on landline phone,
On the other side there was her mom.

She was crying and told to the girl,
Baby your superhero your dad lost his pulse,
It is the time to say him goodbye,
Come back here to give him a last reply.

After hanging up she saw her dad,
Who was smiling looking at her and she felt his hand on her head.

A KING WITH AN INVISIBLE CROWN

I am a rich guy in the town,

I live like a king with an invisible crown,

I have a sport car that moves very fast,
But I was a poor boy in the past.

I do not remind those days now,
I am so famous just say WOW,
But there is something missing,
I generally spend my time in fishing.

There is a boy in my home care staff,
Who tried to be like me superfast,
Who will tell him hard work I did,
How should I tell him that I was not a rich kid.

I also spent my childhood in slum,
Sometimes I need to sleep in a drum,
I was an orphan without mom and dad,
For children like me this world is holy bad.

I used to earn by polish others shoes,
But never missed to read the news,
One day I found country needs some youth,
To go to war and make conditions on the border smooth.
I gave my name to proof my worth,
Might be this is the right reason behind my birth.
Post battle I came back home after 5 years fight,

Now I was a changed person with a future bright.

I got a land from government as a gift for the war,
I started farming on that and bought a car,
With my efforts I started a factory of my own,
I told you earlier I am a king with an invisible crown.

This is my story my whole life,
Now I am living happily with my daughter and a beautiful wife.

KID: THE SUPERHERO

Tick tick my clock says,

And this is Monday again,

Oh I don't want to leave my bed,

God please start the heavy rain.

My family is weird and strange,

Because they shout every time like they are watching a match,

I am a pro player of PUBG,

Because I've learnt it with my game batch.

My mom is in kitchen and daddy is in funny costume,

My sister is shouting where the hell is my German perfume,

God I think I would like to exchange my family today,

I want to replace them with my enemy Emily
who tells everyone that I am a gay.

Oh what kind of life we kid have,

I think we are the real super heroes because no one else is so brave,

Now I am ready to go to the school,

I am so smart but everyone treats me like I am an immatured fool.

I keep the secrets of my sister that she is dating a boy,

In exchange for that I get daily pocket money & robo toy,

What gives me new motivation for the days,

Akon songs in headphones and sun rays.

But I hate to attend the class,

In spite of that I like to see outside of windows glass,

There is a girl who works in a flower shop,

I want to meet her but she works on another side of the road.

I know I am seven but still I have feelings for her,
But without my glasses, everything looks like a blur;
I want to take her on date to the disneyland,
Among all the options, I would always prefer.

But I am scared because of my mom,
She is very strict and blasts everytime like a ticking bomb.
My daddy is cool he will love my bride,
But my elder brother is psycho and always fight,

Oh I forgot here to mention a thing,
That girl is the girlfriend of my brother who thinks he is a king.
How can be she so silly to date a dumb boy like him,
Someone tells her that I am a third class
student and my name is Jim.

This is the best time of every week day,
When we get the middle breaks at noon to play.
Do not tell my secrets to anyone because that is wrong,
I know I am the little one but trust me I am very strong.

WHAT I LEARNED TODAY

Hello everyone I want to invite you all,
Today is my eighth birthday and this is the final call.

My daddy has brought some candies and snacks,
My mom is in the kitchen opening ice cream packs.

I am so excited because I have called my crush,
That is why I have cleaned my teeth with my fav brush.
Today I am going to wear a designer suit,
Because I want to look in my party so handsome & cute.

But I am scared what if my teacher will also attend,
He will tell my result to dad and no one will defend,
Actually I have failed the school exam again,
But I don't want to be a fool in front of my crush and friend.

Do you also celebrate your birthday like me?
My dreams are as endless as the vast blue sea.
But suddenly my parents told me that they have changed the plan,
Daddy said do some help to others whatever you can.

Then we went outside of the town,
There was an orphanage with a beautiful lawn,
My daddy said today we will celebrate your birthday with them,
I became quiet and emotionally withdrawn.

Then my mom told me that these children have no mom & dad,
If I let them join my birthday party they would be glad,

I stopped here and think for a while,
why can I not be the reason for one day for their smile.

I thanked my parents for bringing me here,
I started playing with those children here & there.
Then I cut the cake with everyone including the staff,
For me this birthday was so special and fair.

We do not need to be rich to make someone smile,
We just need to remember humanity for a while,
I wish everyone could help others who really need help,
This is a story about my birthday, almost juvenile.

MY DREAM GIRL

Well well well,

Who is that pretty girl,

Well well well,

Why her hairs are so curl.

She is sitting in the middle of class,

Her skin is shining like a crystal glass.

so I made up my mind that I will learn tricks,

Because speaking without thinking often sounds crass.

From next day onwards my task was to learn manners,

I was feeling like a paper who was going through many scanners.

My friends call me stupid because I fell in love
but I want to show the world,

If my love for her could be written, the
sky would be full of banners.

When one day I thought now I am prepared so well,

I took my granny's car in market to sell,

I got the money and I bought second hand sports bike,

Because she hates cars but likes bike ride.

When I reached to her house I knocked the door twice,

She opened the door and her mouth was full of bread slice.

She was so shocked by seeing me on her door,

She asked me why are you here and I am already so bored.

I told her that I love her so much,

I want to spend my life with her I want to be in touch.

I expressed my emotions by offering a ring,

So that she could understand,
Without her, nothing matters much.

But then I saw my teacher calling my name,
I was surprised what he is doing in her house, what is this game.
Suddenly I opened my eyes, and she was not there,
She left without a word, and I had no one to blame.

Then I understood that I was in a dream,
I wanted to tell her,
Without her love, I'm nothing;
But if I am with her, I rise in esteem.

But teacher suspended me for one month from school,
I wanted to become smart but ended up being a fool.
But I am ready to find my dream girl,
Whose smile is precious, shining brighter than a pearl.

SINGLE GOING TO BE MINGLE

Hello World,

This is my first date,

I am getting ready,
So that I won't be late.

Yesterday a guy asked me for out,
I was surprised and wanted to shout.
Actually I am a poor sales girl,
Who has glasses and hairs are curl.

In high school I was alone,
No one was my friend in school or home,
My parents were lovely but out of funds,
To submit my fee we had to wait for several months.

But I was happy with a positive hope,
One day I will get my love this was my thought,
I completed my studies with highest marks,
But I am not lucky I forgot.

Everyone got placed because of their source,
I belong to a simple family so I bear to this loss,
But I did not give up and went to city,
Now I needed a job with a sweet boss.

I started working in a furniture house,
I started running behind customers like a cat chasing a mouse.

But still I was alone I had not met with my king,
Someone please tell him his queen is waiting for the ring.

But it did not take too long,
A boy proposed to me with a ring and song.
Now my fairy tale is going to be true,
I will be queen only after hours few.

A LOVE STORY

I never thought I will fall in love,

I never thought I will say this to you,

I never thought I will come hereby,

I never thought I would kiss you here.

But when I was working aside,
You were going with your friends seeing a bull fight,
I fallen for you at that time,
My heart starts beating while saying love rhymes.

I followed you there,
To make you mine,
You come in my life like,
Beautiful, lovely sunshine.

Then I came to know that you are sad,
You have lost your dog in city shade,
I got an idea to make you impress,
I started searching for your dog and started to chase.

Somewhere I found that dog with a cat,
He was flirting with her dancing like a brat.
I standing there seeing this beautiful scene,
I hope that someday we will repeat this in the land of green.

Suddenly someone pushed me out of the dream,
I started smiling like I had taken cocaine,
I caught your dog to hand over it to you,

So that I could impress you and ask for a love date too.

When you saw your dog in my lap,
you thought I was a thief and then gave me a slap.
But as you're softhearted and beautiful like snow-white,
You took me into your home and cared for me for a while.

I saw you once again and I felt love,
I asked you for a date and you said no,
My heart again broken into pieces like glass,
I came home and slept on the grass.

Then someone rang my bell twice,
Oh my god It was you with a beautiful smile,
You came with meals and a bottle of wine,
I welcomed you and you sat in my dine.

I told you about my feelings and,
you said you love me too,
I hugged you tightly ,
by saying I love you too.

LOVE CONFESSION

I want to confess,

I want to tell you,

I am in love,

I love you.

But I am scared,
Scared losing you,
I can't live alone,
I planned my life with you.

Just give me a chance,
To be with you,
Accept my love,
and I won't leave you.

Whenever I come,
To tell you about my feeling,
I saw you with others,
my heart stopped beating.

Can you do me a favour,
Just feel my love,
Baby Hug me tight,
like a pair of doves.

We will be together,
and will make our separate space,
You are my life,

No one can ever replace,

I will love you with all my heart,

and we won't ever be apart.

LOVE ME

I like you,

I wanna heal you,

When I am alone,

I wanna feel you.

Sometimes I need love,

Sometimes I need hug,

But when are you with others,

I wanna steal you.

Baby feel me,

Just you heal me,

I am all yours forever,

So you steal me.

CUPID IS SEEING

I show her my lines,

I wrote for her,

She said nothing,

But said that is normal.

That was confession,

In which I proposed,
But she treated me,

Like a mental ghost.

I was very angry,

I was very upset,

How can she be so rude,

By making this statement.

I decided that time,

I will never write for her again,

I will get publish this book,

But on someone else's name.

Never run behind someone,

Who never understood your love,

You will get a better person,

There is a CUPID above,

Now forget your past,

Just smile and move on,

This is your time,

All sorrows have now gone.

Walk on the street ,

With a smile on your face,

Buddy trust me,

Now you look like a BADASS.

SEPARATION

Baby I told you,

never leave me alone,

when you know me well,

then where were you gone.

I saw you going away,
I tried to call you on phone,
You hanged up my call,
and put me in the friend zone.

I never realized,
I never imagined,
You were passing your time,
and I thought you were loving.

I done everything,
to make you happy,
But you played with me,
Like scooby and shaggy.

You said that boy,
was cousin from so far,
But today when I saw,
that in a relationship both you are.

What was my mistake,
That you leaved me,
I was all yours,

then why I am like this in my dream.

You said we will be together forever,
suddenly what happened to you,
why did you break my heart in pieces,
That can never be fixed with any glue.

Now I trust no one,
and I have learnt to live like this,
congrats on your new life,
Mister and miss.

LONELINESS

I am standing with tears in my eyes,

Do I want to end my painful life,

Neither wants someone anymore,

Nor do I have anyone to care for.

When I was alone in the dark,
No one understood me,
but started screaming at me,
Like a Maddy's dog bark.

What could be the reason,
Why everyone hate,
I have never cheated anyone,
I never done gambling and bet.

The girl whom I loved,
She started dating other,
I was on my bed with a fever,
but no one got bothered.

My parents loved my siblings more than me,
I was at home like I was never be,
I called my friends to give me company,
But they said no because I was out of money.

I realised that life is full of shit,
in the last, you get a land of six or seven feet,
I found a job in a hotel around,

I started living alone near a dog pound.

But god was unhappy to see me like this,
So again he played well and blessed me with a stranger's kiss,
She was a girl who was drunk,
She was getting harassed by a roadside punk.

I saved her from him and took her in my home,
She told me she is living here but belongs to Rome,
After some days we started the dating phase,
Then I found her cheating with someone else.

When I asked her the reason she told me that,
She was living with me because she needs a flat,
Once again I was lost and alone,
I was feeling like crying and pain in my bones.

You know what happened after that,
I am standing on this bridge thinking put everything on an end,
Might be I don't have anything or anyone this time,
But I hope after dying I will get a six-foot land.

EMPTINESS

Sometimes I feel like dead,

Sometime I feel alone,

Sometime I hurt myself,

Sometimes I feel like a grown.

How painful is life,
How painful this all,
No one cares for me,
No one makes any calls.

One day I tried to kill me,
But I got saved,
Someone took me hospital,
And I got once again safe.

Now I am taking help of a doctor,
To come out of this depression,
But I don't feel so good,
Nothing is helpful to reduce my tension.

I went to school,
So that I could divert my mind,
But people started making my fun,
This is a harsh reality about human kind.

A girl came so near,
Without any nervousness or fear.
She held my hand,

And took me to her chair.

She told me that,
She wants to be my friend,
She likes me from school,
And wants her life to spend.

I thought it's ending of my sorrow and ending of my pain,
Then I found myself having CPR in a running ambulance van,
Medical team was trying to save me,
But I was dying because I had cut my right hand vein.

So that girl was from my dream,
Who has held my hand,
So this was a story of me,
That has reached an end.

Everyone take care yourself,
Because in reality no one is your friend.

Cheating is not an option

She broke my heart,
And leave me apart,

I asked her so many times,
Believes she is a sweetheart.

But she never loved me,
She never did,
And I was mad about her,
Just like a kid.

When she was alone,
I was with her,
But when I needed her most,
She was busy somewhere.

I told her to,
Not leave me ever,
She promised me that,
She will love me forever.

So I believed,
Like I only need,
Her love, her hug and her love deed.

I never thought,
I will be broken,
Because she entered in my heart,
With VIP token.

I can not blame her,

As she was neat,

I am dying now,

Because I lost my love my each heartbeat.

LIFE IS NOT SAME FOR ALL

I saw her hungry and crying,

her hopes were dying,

the existence of humankind,
was slowly denying.

then I saw a man,
with a knife,
who robbed a man,
threatening his life.

When I went ahead,
I saw a dog,
he was sitting in the car,
in this night full of fog.

Suddenly I felt something close,
shivering bones and runny nose,
that was an old lady ,
who were asking for warm clothes.

When I came back home,
I was sitting on chair,
remembering all those people,
who were dealing differently everywhere.

Now I got the lesson,
that life is not same for everyone here,

People cares for money and status,

and poor lives in hunger and fear.

ONE SIDED LOVE

I saw you once from my window,

That day my mind just blow.

I tried to find you then on my street,

To be friends with you and to greet.

But when I saw you with someone,
My heart was broken and I feel like no one.

I was standing all alone on street,
Like a dead body moving on his feet.

I just want to tell you what I felt that day,
But you had chosen someone and pushed me in hell.

Now when you are happy with him,
I am happy too,
Because love is not only,
To get someone along with you.

SECOND CHANCE

I am sorry baby,

I hurt you so many time,

I never understood your love,

I am sorry for this crime.

Just give me a chance,
To proof I will change,
I will be a better person,
Will together do things to rearrange.

I know I don't deserve baby like you,
You always cared for me but,
I never understood you.

But now I realized our family value,
I am not here to make any new argue,
Just look into my eyes and feel it the way,
First time when we met and you became my bae.

Baby I am incomplete without your love,
I will die soon like an injured dove,
I might lie but my tears won't,
I am ready to write sorry 10000 times in a very big font.

Everyone was right,
I was the person who hurt you most,
I wanted to be your lover ,
but ended up becoming like a torturing ghost.

But just one chance more,
I will fix this thing,
I will impress you again,
I will propose to you with a marriage ring.

LIVE TODAY

I know you are seeing me,

Because you feel for me,

But I don't like,

When someone leave me.

That is why,
I do not need your love,
Just go find someone else,
And let me be tough.

I have learnt to live like this,
I know to survive,
I know what to say,
And when to be quiet.

I have made so many mistakes,
Those put me alive in my grave,
No one wants to listen my story so far,
I am the person with so many scar.

One day people will find my truth,
That what kind of person I was in my youth,
I hurt my parents I cheated my love,
I make my life a hell booth.

Never play with your life,
And take it seriously,
Grow like a tree,
And love your family.

Not all day will be beautiful as you want,
But you will be the writer of story you start,

Never look back and never give away,

Don't worry about the future, just enjoy your day.

LIVE YOUR DREAM

Morning gives me new hope,

Like I am standing in front of the God,

I start my day with a smile,

Because still I need to pass thousands of miles.

Now I don't fear if I go alone,
Because now I know how to live without phone,
People in the world are getting mad,
They are social addicts with millions of waste.

I want to make my own world full of those,
Who don't need to survive on social media dose,
I will fly like a bird in the sky,
My life is not for any pause.

Once I have a bf who was psychopath,
He tried to kill me in a car crash,
Then I realized that people don't love like jerks,
They are just mad for sex, money and drugs.

I came out of my town with my bags,
Started my journey with two black little cats,
I do not have any plan I don't have a map,
I found a wooden cabin to get some nap.

Next day same morning same hope again,
This time I started my journey in a school van,
In middle of a city I met with a guy,

Who wants to hook up with me by offering an apple pie.

I broke his balls and ran away,
Now he will never treat any girl in this way,
Oh my god I just love my life,
This nature's song and this lovely vibe.

I know someday someone will write,
About a girl with two cats and future bright,
Come on you too start living your dream,
You alone are enough not to need a team.

TOGETHER WE LOST

I know I have lost you,

And we won't be together again,

I am here to tell you,

I am gonna miss enjoying the rain.

You were my baby,
We were happy together,
Now when I see old days,
Those seem to be like heartbreakers.

The kitchen which you settled yourself,
The curtain of room and that brown book shelf,
You remember that room that we decorated,
Because as we planned our baby was awaited.

What happened suddenly,
We did not need this change,
Now we are separate,
It seems strange.

Baby come back to me,
So that we could restart,
We will rise once again,
And never gonna be apart.

Do you not want,
To fix the things like before,
We can do it,

As I don't want to live alone anymore.

I am standing out of your home,

Come and see me or just pick my phone.

Baby I am all yours,

And you are mine,

I am never let anyone,

To draw a border line.

I will die or I will proof me,

Baby you are only person who can fix me.

IT'S OKAY TO SAY I'M NOT OKAY

Okay let's end it, if you are bored,

But don't pretend, as you ever cared for.

I am not only who is responsible for this,
You played the same role as I did,
What did you say that day to me,
You want divorce and do not want me.

Now you are telling new story to others,
Telling them that you are a poor girl,
I was the one who trapped you to be with me,
But you forgot that you are the first who kissed me.

Why people react this kind of weird,
It's okay to breakup but never do the hate,
Oh! girl I know how bad you are,
You are planning to legally get my home and car.

If you are a player then I will be a coach,
Either say sorry or change your approach,
Now will you hire a contract killer to kill,
Baby I do not care. I am sleeping after taking the pill.

Welcome abroad as you are in my dream,
Please take your own time but do not scream,
If you want to go out there is just a switch,
I saw you as an angel but you finished this as a Witch.

My friends warned me when I started dating you,
They showed me many times how frustrating was you,
But as I was mad for your love like a baby boy,
As a baby boy never leaves his new toy.

I forgot that time to behave like a grown,
I made you my queen and offered you a crown,
After that you started treating me like your slave,
You do bad things in my bedroom and I will live in a cave.

Oh! please stop, pack your stuff and get out soon,
Baby now forget me and our honeymoon.

THE POOKY BABY GIRL

When I was a kid I was very polite,

But I did not let my parents sleep calmly at night,

I was not sure if I was a good baby of them,

But my daddy used to call me pooky and
mumma kept my name Snowwhite.

I was good in academics and I was good in sports,
My daddy is a lawyer so I used to go with him to visit the courts,
My mom was a piano teacher who was very gentle,
Children always need guidance that is parental.

I took admission in high school in my city,
I was popular on my campus because I was so pretty,
I promised my daddy that I will focus on studies,
But I got diverted from my goals and started doing things so pitty.

When slow time flies and I got so many backs in the class test,
I was scared now because now parents will
cancel my visit to the fest,
So I made a plan to cheat on my mom and dad,
To show them fake results so that they would be glad.

This was the first time when I started
doing bad things in my home,
I just want to prove that my childhood days are gone,
After that day I started ignoring my parents everytime,
I started avoiding their texts and calls on my phone.

I have a boyfriend with whom I did wrong
things on different place,

once who was a topper now cannot show her face,

But still I was not aware that I am playing with my life,

I was thinking that I am creating a fairy
world in my personal space.

One day I insulted my daddy in front of my boyfriend,

I told him that whatever our relation is, that is now end,

His eyes were wet and he was taking my
name in a hampering voice,

But still I asked him to leave right now by
making the wrong choice.

One day, I felt that I was seriously stuck in
the worst part of my story,

I started crying by remembering my childhood memory,

I was pregnant and my boyfriend left me in the apartment alone,

Now I was missing my parents and wanted to say Sorry.

Suddenly I lost my consciousness and fainted down,

A girl is pregnant without marriage, this was the
headlines in the morning in that town,

When I opened my eyes I was lying on a hospital bed,

So I desperately started calling my mom & dad.

I saw them standing on the door, my mom bought
some fruits from the nearby store,

I was feeling so ashamed to face dad, because I knew

my behavior broke him and made him sad.

But still both of them are here with me in my tough time,

But I was not sure how to apologize to them for my serious crime,

Today I realised that parents are really God living with us,

Their blessings are precious and their
presence makes our lives prime.

TOXIC PEOPLE AROUND ME

My life is full of pain,

Now I don't care for what I lose or what I gain,

I have forgot those people,
Who were just like toxic cane.

I shouted a loud,
And warned all,
Never mess with me,
No more texts and no call.

If you want to be happy,
You need to leave everyone,
Nothing is difficult,
It's like chewing and spitting your bubble gum.

Now move ahead,
And find the holes,
Where you could fit your,
All incomplete goals.

Now Go to your room,
Take a shower,
We need to go down,
So put a t-shirt and lower.

I will show you,
Reality of the world,

How they treat others,
With their harsh word.

No need to fear,
No need to cry,
What will you lose now,
When your new home is sky.

Cross your fingers,
And make a wish,
Then go to the last,
And let the people miss.

This is a game,
Where people simply blame,
They forget their actions,
But trap others by taking their name.

Did you do this oh my friend,
Did you also follow this trend,
Let me make you free from your pain,
Just allow me to put this to an end.

BROKEN WINGS

I was so confused,

I was so scared,

Everything was getting vanished,

And I could not stop.

My life was going through ups and downs,
It was getting more worse,
I was losing hopes,
It felt like I was cursed.

I started dreaming about my death,
I was losing god's side and the faith,
I think I was on a wrong road,
No one was there to show me the right path.

No support I got from my friends and all,
They started avoiding my texts and call,
I was a bird with a broken wing,
I was a poor guy who wanted to be king.

I was losing family I was losing my love,
I was losing my identity and is there someone above,
Few of my known people asked me to take loan,
When I applied for the same I got no response.

I needed to submit my fees in the college,
But there were not any single penny in my wallet,
I had final year exams that I needed to attend,

I desperately started finding a job even in a taxi stand.

My parents had already done so many things for me in past,
I was only their child who was born with no talent or no art,
My siblings were settled they were earning so high,
I was sitting alone in my room and started crying.

At a moment I decided to commit suicide,
Then I realized that this was not the
solution that seems to be right,
I stood up on my feet and came out of room,
I decided that I will find a job soon.

Once again I was ready to do the fight back,
Never lose your hope for god sake.

HIDDEN PAIN

I want to tell,

I don't want to lie,

I have lost everything,

My pain is so high.

Don't listen my story,
That is full of glory,
But now everything changed,
And for this I am sorry.

Now I am alone,
My happy days are gone,
No one is mine,
My home is my dead zone.

I fight with my fortune,
Bcz I liked superheroes costume,
But I am of no use,
That's why I don't like June.

I give up today,
I can not rise up again,
I am sorry mom and dad,
I failed both of you again.

INCOMPLETE HOPE

I am walking alone in the dark,

Because I have lost my way and lost my spark,

I wanna fly,

fly in the sky,

But I have lost my wings,
So can never touch so high.

I do remember when I was a kid,
I was so happy, my life was not much rigid,
I went to school to study hard,
So that I become a boss with a bodyguard,
But I started playing cards in the club,
I lost everything and I had no choice but to accept the drub.

Now I am roaming around my parents home,
Tonight I am leaving permanently for Rome,
But I don't have guts to face them once again,
It's something like I am standing in acid rain.

But I promised myself I will take rebirth soon,
Then I won't hurt my parents and I will touch the moon,
I will see new dreams and recreate my wings,
Bcz mom says don't be afraid to get big swings.

I KNOW I HURT YOU

I could not say you mine,

I could not stop the time,

I could not express my pain,

I could not use my brain.

This happened to me,
This happened to my life,
I lost my way,
I could not overcome every strife.

I wanted to be yours forever,
But I could not hold my word,
Because I forgot your value,
I reacted like an angry bird.

Baby forgive me please,
Come back to me again,
I promise I won't repeat this because,
After the storm, flowers bloom in the gentle rain.

I will love you till my last breath,
I will be there whenever you need,
I won't fight, I won't argue,
I will be yours by following your lead.

I will cook daily,
I will cook delicious meals,
You need to come home early,

Because love is the power that always heals.

One day we have a baby like you,
That baby will surely copy whatever you do,
You will change her diaper and I will sleep,
Because a mother needs rest so daddy needs baby to keep

She will grow fast day by day,
I know you will treat her like a morning ray,
She will start dancing with you on your favourite song,
Because true relations remain a treasure lifelong.

It's a story of us,
We are a family of ten,
We have a sports car,
We also own a family van.

MY PAST VS MY PRESENT

I am standing on my terrace thinking to jump and finish my life,

I have tried all way before even I cut my veins with an old knife,

I know you want to know the story behind this scene,

But for that you need to turn the old pages of my life.

I was a dreamer with a dream to join a medical stream,

I want to be a doctor it's my childhood dream,

I prepared myself for a long time,

Saving lives makes a doctor's duty truly supreme.

My dad supported me so hard and went against everyone,

Because people think that girls should
stay home having great fun,

I was standing alone with my dad,

I looked around but except him I found none.

Finally, I starting preparation and left my
mobile that act like a spam,

I prepared day and night for my medical exam,

I don't know why I could not crack it all,

My dreams were shattered on the floor with my fall.

I broke my father's trust and lost all of his hope,

My dad scolded me and said marry to a
man who own a medical shop,

My brother said I am involved with boys
and blamed me for my failure,

I asked him for help, but he said nope.

After convincing my parents they decided
to send me to another state,

Where I started working in a company to change my fate,

But another side I was involved in wrong things,

I was hooking up with guys, because I had
a manipulating roommate.

She told me the easiest way to earn a lot of money,

I was confused first because the idea was so funny,

I had to make several relationships with random online guys,

You know flowers bloom bright when the day is sunny.

I turned to be a bad girl and started flirting in my office and class,

I didn't have an idea that I will lose everything in the last,

I started enjoying these things until I
ended a night in a hotel room,

I had lost that thing that belonged to only my groom,

The boy was on bed next to me,

I was now crying alone because without
marriage I celebrated a honeymoon.

After that day the boy started using me for his pleasure,

I started remembering those days when for
parents I was their priceless treasure,

There are so many girls who are going through the same pain,

They also lose everything with hope of something to gain.

But today I met true love of my life,

He trusts me completely and I am speaking
to him continuously lie,

I don't want to hurt him like this because he
loves me more than I deserve,

I want to spend my life with him, but it's
okay I will see him from the sky.

This is the story behind today's scenes,

This is the story of most of the girls who
once had very big dreams,

No one in this world cares about us as our parents do,

Always speak from the heart, and your words will stay true.

My ex has sent my private pictures to the love of my life,

Who dreamt to marry me and make me his beloved wife,

I have broken the trust of my parents, my love even my own,

Yesterday I was the topper of my batch and
today I am the bad girl of my town

I don't have another option now to survive,

I will jump from here after counting till five,

I am sorry to everyone who trusted me so much,

I wanted to tell my Darling that I love him so much.

Counting stopped and still am alive,

I got a new life when my true love arrive,
I started crying and touched his feet,
And he hugged me tight and made that moment so sweet.

Today I am tying my knot with him in the marriage hall,
That day he accepted me with all scars and the past,
But I know what I have done in the past,
I lost that thing belonging to him, and I can never recall.

LOVE DOESN'T EXIST

I love you, I adore you,

I need you, I want more you,

I need your hug, I need your kiss,

You are far away, so I deeply miss.

I want to hold you tight,
I want to fight,
I want you to be my morning,
I want you to be the moon of my night.

I am so lonely without you,
Is it my mistake that I red handed caught you,

Am I a thing for you to play,
You were the person who asked me to stay,
Now when I come close to you,
You don't need me; why did you say;

I chose you, I supported you,
I left my home just to be with you,
But you left me broken and alone,
Just tell me the reason why you have gone.

Without you I am incomplete,
We will sort everything, let's meet,
Why are you not answering my phone,
Come back to me fast today is our prom.

I do not know how to bear this pain,
I am crying in this heavy rain,
You promised me you won't leave,
Then how dare you do fraud & cheat.

I told you, I don't have anyone except you,
You just come back and I am ready to accept you,
Why are you not understanding me,
The promise was always safely kept you.

You did hurt me every day,
But you behaved so nice another day,
I was so stupid who trusted you,
Every youth must listen to what elders say.

I cannot believe you were fake,
I know now you are not coming back,
I just want to tell you a thing,
I am also leaving this town next morning,

I also will not keep a single memory of you,
As you forgot me, I will forget you;
Now I decided to live my life alone,
I won't be someone's wife nor will I become mom

This is the best way to punish myself for being wrong,
But still I need to struggle for so long.

Some stories never have a happy ending,
Broken hearts try their best to keep mending,
My tears fall silently, with letters still sending,
But my memories with him are slowly blending.

WRONG ACCEPTANCE

I don't know what is my fault,

I accepted her with her badly past,

First she did hide the truth and married me,

But after marriage her truth is coming out so fast.

She played an emotional game,
She told herself a victim and started others to blame,
She said she was trapped in so deep,
Memories of the past are hard to keep.

She said she was so innocent to trust her ex and friends,
But suddenly her life took many unexpected bends,
She did not want to become so bad,
But she started enjoying bad things in the ends.

I thought she was telling me the truth,
Her gentle words were meant to soothe,
I decided to give her another chance,
Because sometimes the world can be cruel and show no ruth.

She was the only one who came to me,
Then she asked gently will you marry me,
I was not aware of her past at the time of our wedding,
Happiness and joy were slowly spreading.

Next day her ex sent her private photos,
Life lessons are often captured in simple mottos,
But when I heard her story I trusted her again,

But I was not aware that she had a different plan.

After accepting her past she started causing quarrel in home,
I broke down inside me and started sitting alone,
Now I was feeling that I have made a wrong decision,
Because day by day she was changing her
behaviour and talking tone.

I cannot tell you how I have spent one year like this,
But if I leave her, I am gonna miss,
So many times I requested her to change,
She replied politely that she would and gave me a kiss.

But every 20 days she starts fighting like before,
Sometimes I feel dying because I can't bear it anymore,
One thing I have better understood about this generation,
To cheat and keep so many relationships
before marriage is new fashion.

But I am not that kind of man,
I feel like I don't belong to this new fashion clan,
She cheated on me and I forgave her,
I keep standing through every storm across the span.

REALITY VS EXPECTATION

I have so much pain in heart of me,

Hoping one day I will truly feel free,

I am sure she will never change,
Sometimes life feels completely strange.

I have decided now I won't say her a single word,
but I have kept all my promises as a beautiful song of bird,
I had a beautiful life which I have ruined and spoiled,
But one day my story will be heard.

I don't know why people keep affairs before marriage,
Facing challenges together required great courage,
You do the wrong things by hiding from your mom and dad,
They always supported you, no matter what they had.

As a husband I completely justified my duties towards my wife,
But she played with my emotions and I hate this life,
She does not want to understand my love and feelings for her,
Maybe she will understand it when I enter my afterlife.

I am getting mad because of her actions,
Her rude behavior often leads to many distractions.
I was preparing for my exams to secure a government job,
But because of all this mess my plan has become a flop,
Before I was a believer of love and God,
But trust me people, this is a new way to do fraud.

MY TRUE LOVE

I met a guy on a matrimonial site,

He said I am pretty and said his name is Alex Bright.

I was feeling shy when I was checking his pics,

He has a masculine body and a CD that is full of classic remix.

He asked me for a date,
I was nervous thinking is it really my fate,
I said yes, that I will come,
He said he will pick me up and won't be late.

I went to parlour having a stylish haircut and face glow,
I want to be like a pop queen like Nicky Minaz or my fav J-Lo,
I was checking my purse that I have money or not,
But I was so lucky that day because I got my bills very low.

Now I have to buy a sexy gown,
The special one, no one wears in the town,
I was feeling like I am a princess,
Princes of dreams without a crown.

Well, he was about to come at nine,
I started wearing my dress and jewellery
to make me glow & shine,
Then I heard a car sound near my garage door,
My heart was beating so fast and I told her, don't worry it is fine.

Then I went with him for a beautiful long drive,
My head was on his shoulder and the first time I was feeling alive,
Then he stopped the car at a beautiful site,

Where no one was present when we arrived.

Suddenly my man came close to me and kissed my forehead,
Tears came in my eyes and I was feeling so glad,
He sat on his knees and started purposing me,
His sudden action made me mad.

I said yes and we got married,
Every dream I held close, carefully carried,
Today I am telling my love story to my first born,
Old days of adventure, in colours so varied.

So friends true love still exists in the world,
Just wait for your time and don't rush by being a nerd,
Love is awesome when it finds you by itself,
Moments of joy spun around and whirled.

FEAR TO LOSE HIM

I lost my husband in an accident and I became a single mom,

Somehow I started earning to manage my home,

I had the best husband who truly loved me from his heart,

He used to kiss my forehead saying morning my sweetheart.

He always cared for me more than anyone else,
Whenever I used to see him I felt so blessed,
We were enjoying our life full of dreams,
We used to share at night the funny memes.

He always told me that I am the only reason for his smile,
We kept walking together for quite a mile,
I felt safe whenever I held his hand,
He was my everything and a best friend.

I never imagined my life without him,
The news about the accident was truly grim,
He was in front of me without having any heartbeat,
Every moment with him felt so sweet.

By losing him all sudden I have lost all hope,
Sometimes it's hard to manage and cope.
I cry every night by remembering him close to me,
He was the reason I opened my eyes every morning to see.

He has made my life beautiful by sacrificing all his dream,
Please come back to me, I want to scream,
He was driving that day to bring me flowers and a present,

I loved his voice because his speech had a charming accent.

I am ready to die in his place,
I just want to see again his smiling face,
I never had anything mine till the time we met,
Every detail of the day I'll never forget.

He was in the airport to pick someone up,
It seems that nature created everything like this as a setup,
The person for whom he was waiting was already left,
And I was there for my ride to pick up.

I got a cancellation text from my booking app,
I was so tired and wanted to have a nap,
As there was no taxi available that busy time,
I gently asked him to drop me nearby wearing a funny cap.

He was polite so he gave me a lift towards the taxi stand,
I was nervous so he said treat me as your friend.

I was new in the city and did not know anyone,
But driving with him was really fun,
Then he dropped me in a taxi stand,
Finally, this beautiful riding has an end.

As I was new I needed to find a hostel or paying guest,
I mentioned earlier I was so tired so I needed a rest.

But when he heard this he offered to stay at his home,
He said he has two sisters, one brother, dad and mom,
Initially I was sceptical as he was a stranger,
Going with him tonight might be a danger.

But suddenly his phone rang and he picked up the call,
I took his phone hoping to catch a glimpse beyond the wall,
It was his mom talking to me other side,
She invited me home, and we started a new ride.

I got so much love from them like my own family do,
Then I realised my feelings for him were true,
We dated for a month and fell in love,
The stars shine brightly high above.

But see today I have lost the reason to survive,
Our love story started from a long drive.

Suddenly I heard he whispered calling out my name,
Life sometimes feels like a complicated game,
But when I opened my eyes I was in his arms,

On the cold night of winter, I was feeling so warm.

I started crying badly and told him about what I saw,
But this moment of magic, flawless without a flaw,
He held me tight and promised he wouldn't ever leave,
He will be with me forever; I just need to believe.

MY PROFESSIONAL JOURNEY

Come everyone let me tell you a story,

But listen to it carefully & if I am wrong then I am sorry,

It's about my day in the office and my job,

Trust me folks it is not just mine but every workers' story.

I passed my degree with the highest marks in my batch,

Dreams were waiting, just a spark to catch,

I was so excited to work to make my all dreams true,

Opportunities came fast, I had to snatch.

I got a job soon in a very big firm,

My confidence grew as mentors would affirm,

I decided that I will crack every deal,

Every deal had a start and an ending term.

In beginning of job I enjoyed a lot,

Including training period and flirting with colleagues in parking lot,

Life was going so smoothly just like a Lamborghini car,

I am a long race horse so I will go so far.

After the training when I hit the floor,

Oh my god what happened to me why my life turned from sweet to sour,

I started working from nine to nine,

My gf left me by telling me she is not ready to be mine.

Initially my life seemed to be a fairy tale,

I was the prince of my dream and every
moment was told in rich detail.

Everyone was happy under my beautiful wings,

Now the king would rise as people shouted hail.

But suddenly reality hit my mind,

Before and after the academic journey life is of a different kind,

I thought in college that I will earn in millions,

oh no money in my pocket, please excuse and let me find.

Those who thinks that they are working in big companies,

I just want to tell you, guys you are still a slave,

Your bosses are earning huge because of
you but see what they gave,

But what can we do, we are out of funds,

We have a business idea chasing our
dreams, we went on long runs,

Is this the real freedom our ancestors wanted for us all,

Hope kept them warm beneath the bright suns.

Just think all this by sitting alone,

Start writing your story by putting your earphone,

Feel the winds and songs of your inner soul,

Life is a match where sometimes we win,
sometimes it ends with a foul.

But that does not mean giving it up here,

Act like a fox and stop being a professional owl.

NEW BEGINNING

Oh come to me oh come on honey,

Don't lose your hope dreams may hop like a bunny,

Sometimes you rise and sometimes you fall,

But nothing is permanent even tough days can feel so funny.

Look chase your dreams do not lose your hope,
Just follow your goals like in rome many people follow the Pope,
Hurdles can be tough and they can seem too big,
But you need to find another way as there is a big scope.

This is your life this is your game,
If today you keep fighting you will win and will get so much fame,
Today everyone makes fun of you and let them do the same,
When you will be on top they will survive on your name.

I know this is so hard in the initial phase of the fight,
But you will learn with every step you count today till midnight,
You are not doing this for others or for anyone you know,
Because once you accept your worth and
your future will be bright.

We all are warriors we all are fighters in our inner space,
To feel it inside you live the life but don't make it a race,
Do not play with your emotions do not play with your heart,
You just need to think about yourself and
you have dreams to chase.

I know I might be wrong sometime,
But I am a poet and I keep my poem making it a rhyme,

Just like me you can also live your dream,

Just think and start because the signal is already green.

FATHER - THE UNSUNG HERO

Today I will tell you a story of a father daughter and a son,

Both children are starting to grow as planets shine under the sun,

You need to feel the emotions of a father
who doesn't show his tears,

Trust me this story is not fake but a heart touching one.

When someone becomes a father he decides to be forever strong,

He might be a smart bunny but he needs
to act now as a King Kong,

He starts thinking about his family by sacrificing his all wishes,

And he does the same for everyone in the family for so long.

He works so hard in his job to fulfil your need,

He returns home with so much pain in his body and in the feet,

But when his family comes close to him to play and talk,

He acts normal by hiding his pain and daddy this is a cheat.

We don't understand the value of our father in our life,

We forget what our parents has sacrificed
for us when we get our wife,

Why do we not understand the pain our father hide,

Why no one cares about his sacrifices he
has made in his whole life.

If you want to know the value of a father
ask who does not have one,

Without father life will become so dark like
a planet without having a sun,

But still we do not care for his dream and hope,

He sat in the corner alone and began to mope.

What is his fault what has he done so wrong,
You hurt him so many times but still in his heart he will always belong,
You forget your childhood days you have spent with him in his lap,
How did he change your mood from upset to happy by singing a song?

Mother and father are not less than a real god,
They only truly care about you without being a fraud,
This is the time go and touch feet of them,
Say sorry to them and fix the broken family picture frame.

Mom can reduce her pain by her tears or sharing it with others,
She discusses every problem with her sisters & brothers,
But father can't be weak so he can't show his pain by making his eyes wet,
He always comes in between you and your cruel fate.

Look, this story cannot get an end,
Do not treat your father like unknown but treat him like a friend,
If you believe in God Then God is in your parent’s blessings,
So it’s better to be real to them than just pretend.

PARENTS ARE REAL GOD

I was in school and enjoying my life,

I made new friends and we did hunting night,

I spent my whole day chilling with the chicks,
On the other side my parents were earning hard by making bricks.

But they never make me feel this pain,
So I never understood how hard to work for a penny in heavy rain,
My mother cleaned utensils in other's home,
Dad was a labourer who was suffering from down syndrome.

Still both of them were working hard,
Here I lost and forgot my past,
There were many days when My parents
remain hungry to feed me,
But today I am wasting my time when they need me.

How can a child forget his parent's effort,
How they grow their kids by making them an expert,
But when we grow we treat them bad,
We take their names but do not call them mom and dad.

Trust me guys you are gonna loose,
Something that is precious but you did not choose.
There is time to accept your mistakes and say sorry for harassing,
Go apologize to your parents and ask for their precious blessings.
Value your parents if you do not want to guilt,
Because after losing them you will lose everything they built.

Do not forget sacrifices they have made,
They slept on the ground but gave you a bed.

When you were eating cheese and meat,
They were busy thinking how income and expenses will meet,
When you were asking for new books,
You father worked overtime and lost his younger looks.

When you were started dating a chick,
Your mom was waiting for her medicine to buy next week.
You were wasting the time and money,
Here your parents were working hard for a penny.

Get up my friend it's time to tribute them,
Do not play like a kid and don't take this life as a game.

OUR PROTECTORS

We are safe and we are happy in our homeland,

Do we really have an idea who is on the border for us to defend,

We enjoy our home by spending time on phone & internet,

But a soldier fights for us every moment till the very end.

We are so rude we have forgotten the story of our past,
How our nation was divided on the basis of status & cast.
Everyone was a slave, everyone was dying,
People were starving and babies were sleeping and crying.

By sacrificing so many lives we got our freedom one day,
But for our pain and tears who will pay,
It took so much to stand once again,
Success favours those who use their brain.

Our leaders came front to make our nation strong,
But still we are developing just tell me how long,
Our soldiers were out of funds & guns,
They were hungry living on the border
dependent on tea and buns.

Today we are busy in our bogus life full of non-sense things,
Sometimes we are addicted to social media,
sometimes we run behind marriage rings.

Just think once about those who are protecting us from others,
Do not forget we all are brothers from different mothers.
Without them you will die soon that is a true fact,
Respect them because your small efforts can make a huge impact.

So many soldiers have lost their lives just
to defend us in tough times,

You can't write a song for them but at
least for them, read a rhyme.

I know you all love your flag and motherland,

So write so many letters to the soldiers with respect and just send,

Our nation is safe our flag is rising so high,

Because some people on the border are
acting like satellites in the sky.

I AM A SOLDIER

Though I stumbled and felt I might fail,

I assumed this world was a dangerous sea and I am a whale.

In every step I found my soul,

Through broken pieces, I became whole,
Whenever I feel I am drowning in the sea,
I always tried to keep my mind in control.

Initially stage I was scared of the crowd,
But now everyone steps back when I say my name so loud.
I love my nation and I always wear an army tag,
I used to carry with me our national flag.

I know this is not the right time,
I am making jokes and a rhyme.
Oh in front of me there is a tank coming down the hill,
I will play with it, this situation is full of thrill.

If today on this border I die protecting my home,
A place of warmth where I'm never alone.
I have so many friends who are in the mood to play,
Enemies you need to change your plan for the remaining day.

There is a letter in the left pocket my friend,
If I die today, you need it to send,
Tell my family I fought bravely without fear,
If my parents start crying just tell them I hate tears.

Assure them I will take rebirth soon,

Then I will spend my day with dad and will hear
the story from mom beneath the moon,

Then you will see a lady crying in the corner of our hut,

What should I say to her, I don't have that guts.

She is that girl who decided to live with me her whole life,

Everyone tried to convince her not to marry me and be my wife.

But she avoided all and held my hand,

And said I will wait for you till the very end.

So I think this is the last page of my story,

I will return soon covered in glory.

Papa, I will miss my village and old time,

Please don't cry and don't make my sacrifice a painful rhyme.

NEW DOG IN THE TOWN

Hello folks meet me now,

I am a pet and I bark bow bow.

I have a friend whose name is Sam,
He used to play daily with me game.

I love to eat and love to walk,
I enjoy playing and talking for a long talk.
I am naughty so I tease everyone,
It's my way to make daily fun.

I was adopted as I was in shelter,
But every moment with this family made life better.
But I am not alone here who is a dog,
I have a little brother Rio who is white as fog.

I am black and my name is phoenix,
I enjoy listening to and dancing on DJs remix.

I love when someone calls my name,
I am smart so I shake my hands with them,
I used to run all over the house,
I like to chase birds and mouse.

I can't speak like humans do,
But with my actions I say I love you,
I am so loyal like no one is,
My connection with family is so true.

Do you have a dog like my family own,
You adopt too from shelter in the town,
We will play when you will be free,
Like waves dancing endlessly in the sea.

HOW PEOPLE SEE OLD PEOPLE

I am weak now and I am old,

But once at a time I was so bold,

Today people treat me like a burden,
I just need to sit quietly, my grandson told.

Why do people forget that they will face this phase,
Life has a game for everyone like a complicated maze,
No one wants to live with us in our own home,
They throw us out to survive making us alone.

What kind of behaviour do you guys show,
Don't forget that with old parents your fate will grow,
You treat us like we don't exist in your life,
Because you think we are old, weak and slow.

We have made sacrifices to give a life you have,
But in return of that what you gave,
We don't ask your money we don't need your car,
Just sit with us for a while and don't live so far.

We need your love, we ask for care,
Today we are retired but we made you a player,
Have you forgotten how much pain your
mom bear when you were born,
Do not make her heart feel broken and torn.

Today you mention you have to pay my bills,
You forgot who taught you those household skills,

You tell your mom that she does not fit in your league,
I can't see her crying, do not hurt her please.

I am a man so I will pass this time,
But she is your mom in every joy and every crime,
How can you be so arrogant and so rude,
You think you are educated by saying hello dude.

We just want to see our children happy and grow,
Childhood, younger days and old age is just a time flow,
We will leave this world one day,
But God bless you this is our permanent pray.

Do not treat us like a garbage bag,
Don’t let worries and sadness drag,
Do not forget I am your dad and she is your mom,
I am the roof and she is the soul of the home.

MY PAIN OR MY PEN

Sometimes we need a hand to hold tight,

Sometimes we love the day more than a night,

Sometimes we lost in the crowd of thousands,

Sometimes we prefer dark in place of light.

This is not just a poem this is the pain,
These are my words I have written with my pen,
I don't know why I cannot sleep peacefully at night,
If you want to know me then listen I am a broken man.

I don't know what to write in other pages,
Because this time I am going through so many emotional phases,
I am alone and no one is there to talk,
No one is there to hold me or go for a walk.

I don't have expectations I just need the peace,
Do not call my name, don't bother me please,
I have lost in mid of my storybook,
I forgot I am Peter Pan or Captain Hook.

Look, do not call doctor for my checkup,
Because I planned differently than the Gods setup,
I am a writer who is struggling to connect with the crowd,
But my life is still covered with the black clouds.

Writers create stories that connect people with their inner soul,
In God's story we all must play our proper role,
Do not worry if you forget your script,

Just read the next chapter so slowly scroll.

I was so curious to know my future predictions,
I have no job, money and gf but have so many rejections,
My mom says I look like an actor,
She acts as a guardian and a protector.

My daddy says keep patience and never stop to try,
Keep yourself motivated and touch the sky,
How I tell them I am of no use,
My confidence feels fragile and I'm gonna lose.

It is a sad story of a broken pen and old book,
In place of a writer I should start working as a cook,
People tell that I write in old writing style,
Even in my serious poems people laugh and smile.

Today I have decided I won't write any further poem or story,
Those who have expectations from me, look I'm sorry,
I have signed up for a new LinkedIn account,
Every lesson in life felt truly paramount.
What are you waiting for, the poem has already ended,
But this last book is for everyone highly recommended,
Do not think am smart, or I am playing well,
I will keep moving forward along the long trail.

HAPPY ENDING

So this is the last emotion of this book,

Everyone loves reading in a quiet nook,

Someone enjoyed it but someone cried,

Some people miss the chance and they never took.

I tried to cover everyone's emotions in very short,
Thank you readers for your love & Support,
Writing is my passion & I am still learning this art,
In this book I tried to pour my pure heart.

I tried my best to connect with everyone,
So these poems are written for entertainment and fun,
Whenever you read take coffee or wine,
Because there are hidden emotions in each line.

Every ending hides a painful start,
To rhyme it properly I have ignored the grammar part,
No one knows why I wrote this book,
Our stories could fill a tragic chart.

Words might be imaginary but emotions are true,
Just read it alone and it will connect with you,
These are stories those are hard to tell,
But I will listen to them, you just need to mail.

This is not the last message from me,
I will keep writing till I feel free,
If you have suggestions or you want to share review,

I'll be here to listen and create something new.

So now I need your permission to finish this story,

For all the mistake, again I want to say sorry,

I am glad that you walked with me together till this page,

I tried leaving a story behind that no one can erase.

"FINISH"

"Thank you for walking with me through these Silent Harmonies. May the echoes of these verses stay with you, long after the last page is turned."

- Karan Samrat

---

www.ingramcontent.com/pod-product-compliance
Ingram Content Group UK Ltd.
Pitfield, Milton Keynes, MK11 3LW, UK
UKHW041317190726
13845UKWH00025B/342

9 789334 421750